Presented To

_____

By

_____

On

_____

ZONDERKIDZ

The Beginner's Bible® People of the Bible
Copyright © 2018 Zondervan
Illustrations © 2016, 2018 Zondervan

Requests for information should be addressed to:
Zonderkidz, 3900 Sparks Dr. SE, Grand Rapids, Michigan 49546

ISBN 978-0-310-76503-5

Written by: Laura Smith
Illustrations: Denis Alonso
Design: Diane Mielke

Printed in China

18 19 20 21 22 23 24 25 / LPC / 15 14 13 12 11 10 9 8 7 6 5 4 3 2 1

The Beginner's Bible

People of the Bible

ZONDERkidz
.com

Contents

Old Testament

Contents

New Testament

Adam and Eve

Adam and Eve were the very first people. God created Adam from dust.

God wanted Adam to have a best friend. So God made Eve from one of Adam's ribs.

God created both Adam and Eve in his
image. That means God made Adam and
Eve to act like him and love like him. God
loved Adam and Eve very much.

God planted a beautiful garden called
Eden. Adam and Eve lived there. Adam
and Eve took care of all the animals in
Eden. They walked and talked with God
in the garden.

9

Takeaway:
You were made in God's image too. That means you were created to act and love like God.

So God created human beings in his own likeness. He created them to be like himself. He created them as male and female. God blessed them. —Genesis 1:27–28

Prayer:
Dear God, thank you for making me to be like you. Amen.

Fun Fact

Adam and Eve made the first clothes out of fig leaves.

Fun Fact

All of us are related to Adam and Eve. They are our great, great, great, great (too many greats to count) grandma and grandpa.

Fun Fact

God let Adam name all the animals.

Read the Whole Story: Genesis 1–3

Noah

Noah always listened to God, even
when other people didn't. Noah was
kind and good when everyone else
was being mean and bad. So God
decided to save Noah.

God gave Noah a big job to do. God told
Noah to build a giant boat called an ark.

Noah's job was hard work. People
made fun of Noah because there was
no water for his boat. But Noah didn't
give up. He built the ark anyway,
because God asked him to.

Noah listened to God, and God saved
Noah and his family from the flood.

Takeaway:
It doesn't matter what other people do. Always listen to God. He will take care of you.

Then the LORD said to Noah, "Go into the ark with your whole family. I know that you are a godly man among the people of today."
—Genesis 7:1

Prayer:
Dear God, thank you for keeping me safe during scary and stormy times. Amen.

Fun Fact

The ark was as long as 1-1/2 football fields and as tall as a four-story building.

Fun Fact

Noah was 500 years old when he became a father to his three sons. Their names were Shem, Ham, and Japheth.

Fun Fact

When the flood was over, the ark landed on Mount Ararat.

Read the Whole Story: Genesis 6–9

Abraham

Abraham trusted God. God promised
to give Abraham a big family. His
family would become an entire nation!
But first, God told Abraham to go on a
journey to a new and different place.

Abraham's wife was named Sarah.
Abraham and Sarah packed everything
they owned and left their home. Abraham
and Sarah's journey was hard. Some days
they didn't have enough food. Some days
they were strangers in new places.

Abraham and Sarah traveled for hundreds of miles. But Abraham always trusted God's promise. He knew God would bring him where he should go.

God led Abraham and Sarah to Canaan.
Canaan was a wonderful land full of
food and water. It was a perfect home
for Abraham, Sarah, and the family God
gave them.

Takeaway:
Trust God. He will take care of you.

Abram believed the LORD. The LORD was pleased with Abram because he believed. So Abram's faith made him right with the LORD.
—Genesis 15:6

Prayer:
Dear God, please help me always trust you, no matter what! Amen.

Fun Fact

Abraham had his son, Isaac, when he was 100 years old!

Fun Fact

Abraham's name was Abram. God changed it to Abraham, which means "father of many nations."

Fun Fact

Abraham was a rancher. His job was raising animals.

Read the Whole Story: Genesis 12–25

Sarah

Sarah was Abraham's wife. God
promised to give them a big family,
and Sarah trusted God too.

Sarah wanted a baby. But she was an old woman. After waiting for years and years, Sarah worried that she would never have the family God promised her.

But God had a big plan. He kept his
promise to Sarah. Sarah had a son
when she was ninety years old! She
named her son Isaac.

Isaac had kids and grandkids and great grandkids. The entire Hebrew nation came from Abraham, Sarah, and Isaac. Just like God promised.

Takeaway:
God keeps his promises, even when they sound impossible.

"I will give her my blessing. You can be sure that I will give you a son by her. I will bless her so that she will be the mother of nations. Kings of nations will come from her." —Genesis 17:16

Prayer:
Dear God, help me remember that you keep your promises. Amen.

Fun Fact
God changed Sarah's name at the same time he changed Abraham's name.

Fun Fact
Sarah's name used to be Sarai.

Fun Fact
When God told Abraham that Sarah would have a son, she laughed out loud.

Read the Whole Story: Genesis 12–23

Rebekah

Rebekah loved to help others.

When a traveler asked Rebekah for some water, Rebekah helped him. Rebekah got water from a well and shared it with the traveler.

She even got water for the traveler's camels!

The traveler needed a place to sleep.
So Rebekah invited him to her
family's house. Rebekah had a great
place for his camels to stay too.

The traveler was Abraham's servant.
Because Rebekah was so kind and
helpful, he asked Rebekah to come with
him and marry Isaac. She agreed to go
and become Isaac's wife.

Rebekah was a helpful wife to Isaac.
Many years later, Rebekah helped her
son Jacob too.

Takeaway:
God helps us in many ways. He wants us to help others whenever we can.

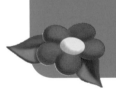

"Will you go with this man?" "Yes, I'll go," she said. —Genesis 24:58

Prayer:
Dear God, please help me help others. Amen.

Fun Fact

Abraham's servant gave Rebekah a nose ring and two gold bracelets as presents.

Fun Fact

God told Rebekah her sons would each start their own nation.

Fun Fact

Rebekah had twin sons, Jacob and Esau.

Read the Whole Story: Genesis 24–27

Jacob

Rebekah's son, Jacob, was
amazed by God.

God gave Jacob a dream about angels
going up and down a staircase to heaven.
When Jacob woke up, he said,
"Incredible! Wonderful!"

Right away, Jacob built an altar to
worship God. He wanted to show others
how great God is.

Jacob became very rich. He had a
large family and hundreds of sheep
and goats. Jacob praised God for
everything he had. Jacob even praised
God when bad things happened,
because God gave him so many
blessings.

When Jacob was worried or frightened,
he talked to God.

In good and bad times, Jacob would say,
"Mighty is the God of Israel."

Takeaway:
Jacob praised God for everything that happened to him. Everything good comes from God.

"God has given me so much. I have everything I need." —Genesis 33:11

Prayer:
Dear God, thank you for all the awesome things you do for me.
Amen.

Fun Fact
One night Jacob had a wrestling match with God!

Fun Fact
Jacob's name means "he grabs the heel." When Jacob and his twin, Esau, were born, he was holding Esau's heel.

Fun Fact
God gave Jacob a new name, Israel, so that Jacob would never forget the wrestling match.

Read the Whole Story: Genesis 25–35

Joseph

Joseph was sent to a lot of places
he didn't want to go. But God used
Joseph to do good things everywhere
he went.

Joseph was taken away to Egypt to be a slave. Then Joseph was thrown into jail, even though he didn't do anything wrong.

Later, Joseph worked for Pharaoh.

God told Joseph there would not be enough food for seven long years. So Joseph helped Pharaoh store food. That way, people wouldn't go hungry.

Joseph's brothers came to Egypt to
find food. Joseph gave them food, jobs,
and homes in Egypt. His family had
everything they needed.

Takeaway:
You can make a difference everywhere you go.

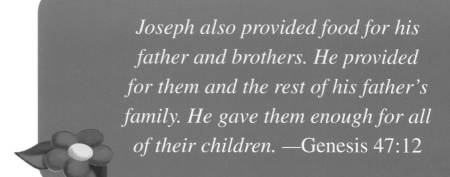

Joseph also provided food for his father and brothers. He provided for them and the rest of his father's family. He gave them enough for all of their children. —Genesis 47:12

Prayer:
Dear God, please help me do good things everywhere I go. Amen.

Fun Fact
Joseph's dad gave him a beautiful robe.

Fun Fact
Joseph had ten older brothers.

Fun Fact
With God's help, Joseph could explain what people's dreams meant.

Read the Whole Story: Genesis 37–48

Moses

Moses persevered. That means Moses didn't give up.

God told Moses to ask Pharaoh to free
the Israelites from Egypt. "Let my people
go!" Moses told Pharaoh.

Moses and his brother, Aaron, showed
Pharaoh signs of God's power. God even
turned their walking stick into a snake.
But Pharaoh wouldn't listen.

Moses said to Pharaoh, "If you don't
free God's people, God will cover
your land with frogs." The frogs came.
They were everywhere! But Pharaoh
still wouldn't listen.

God had Moses send swarms of bugs,
heaps of hail, darkness, and even worse
things to show Pharaoh God's power.
Moses never gave up until Pharaoh freed
the Israelites.

Takeaway:
Moses never gave up. God can help you keep trying, even when it's hard.

Say to Pharaoh, 'The LORD, the God of the Hebrews, has sent me to you. He says, "Let my people go."'—Exodus 7:16

Prayer:
Dear God, when you ask me to do something, help me never give up. Amen.

Fun Fact

When Moses was a baby, his mom hid him in a basket in the river to keep him safe.

Fun Fact

God gave Moses the Ten Commandments to teach people how to live.

Fun Fact

Moses was nervous about talking to Pharaoh. So God sent Moses' brother, Aaron, to help.

Read the Whole Story: Exodus 1–40

Rahab

Rahab was a brave woman. Rahab
helped God's people when they were
in danger.

When Joshua sent spies into Jericho,
Rahab let them stay in her house.

The king's soldiers came to look for the
spies, but Rahab hid Joshua's friends on
her roof. She sent the soldiers away.

Then, Rahab helped the spies escape town.

The spies were grateful for Rahab's help. So Rahab asked them for a favor. "Will you protect my family?"

When the Israelites came back to take over Jericho, the spies kept Rahab's family safe.

Takeaway:
Rahab was brave and helped God's people.

The LORD your God is the God who rules in heaven above and on the earth below. —Joshua 2:11

Prayer:
Dear God, help me be brave enough to help others for you.
Amen.

Fun Fact
Rahab lowered the spies out her window with a rope.

Fun Fact
When the Israelites came back to Jericho, they knew to protect the family with the red rope in their window.

Fun Fact
The spies moved Rahab and her family to a safe camp nearby.

Read the Whole Story: Joshua 2 and 6

Deborah

Before the Israelites had kings, God
sent judges to rule over them. Deborah
was a judge. She was very wise.

The Israelites asked Deborah many questions. Deborah helped them make decisions.

God gave Deborah a plan to defeat a bad king. Deborah told God's plan to the Israelites.

Deborah knew the right time to attack.
She was the one who cried, "Charge!"
Deborah and the Israelites won the battle.

Takeaway:
God told Deborah the right thing
to do. God will show you what to
do too.

*The Israelites went up to her there.
They came to have her decide
cases for them. She settled matters
between them.* —Judges 4:5

Prayer:
Dear God, please give me wisdom
to know right from wrong. Amen.

Fun Fact
Deborah worked under a palm tree.

Fun Fact
Deborah's husband's name was Lappidoth.

Fun Fact
The people even named the tree The Palm Tree of Deborah.

Read the Whole Story: Judges 4–5

Gideon

Gideon didn't think he could be a mighty warrior.

God sent an angel to tell Gideon, "Go and save Israel."

Gideon was afraid. He didn't think he could save God's people from their powerful enemy. But God told Gideon, "You are strong. I will be with you."

Gideon didn't have a big army. He
didn't have weapons. But Gideon
trusted God. Gideon's men smashed
clay jars, lit bright torches, and blew
trumpets. Their enemies were afraid
and ran away.

Gideon did what God asked him to do,
and God helped Gideon's tiny army win
the battle.

Takeaway:
God helped Gideon do great things. With God, you can do great things too.

The angel of the LORD appeared to Gideon. He said, "Mighty warrior, the LORD is with you."
—Judges 6:12

Prayer:
Dear God, please help me remember that I can do big, important things with your help. Amen.

Fun Fact

Gideon started out with an army of over 30,000 men!

Fun Fact

God shrunk Gideon's army to 300 men. That way, everyone saw that God helped them win.

Fun Fact

Gideon became Israel's fifth judge.

Read the Whole Story: Judges 6–8

Samson

Samson was a judge like Deborah. Samson led the Israelites for twenty years. God gave Samson super strength.

Samson was a Nazirite. A Nazirite was
a person who made a special promise to
serve God. Nazirites never cut their hair.

Samson was so strong, he killed a lion
with only his hands.

Samson was so strong, he could break through ropes if he got tied up. Before Samson died, he used the strength God gave him to knock a building down on God's enemies.

Takeaway:
With God's help, you can do
mighty things.

*Then the Spirit of the LORD came
powerfully on Samson.* —Judges 14:6

Prayer:
Dear God, thank you for giving me
strength to do things I can't do on
my own. Amen.

Fun Fact

Samson wore his long hair in seven braids.

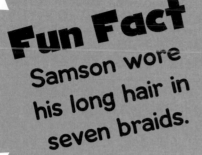

Fun Fact

One time, Samson got very thirsty. God sprayed water from the ground to give Samson a drink.

Fun Fact

Samson liked to tell riddles.

Read the Whole Story: Judges 13–16

Ruth

Ruth was loyal to her family. That means she would do anything for them.

Ruth was married to Naomi's son. But Ruth's husband and Naomi's husband both died. Naomi told Ruth to start a new family of her own. But Ruth would not leave Naomi by herself.

Ruth took care of Naomi. When they were hungry, Ruth gathered leftover grain from a field for them to eat. The owner of the field was named Boaz. Boaz was kind to Ruth.

Boaz fell in love with Ruth. They got married. Ruth and Boaz welcomed Naomi into their home. They became Naomi's new family.

Takeaway:
God wants us to love our families.

Where you go I'll go. Where you stay I'll stay. Your people will be my people. Your God will be my God. —Ruth 1:16

Prayer:
Dear God, thank you for my family. Help me love them well.
Amen.

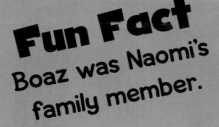

Fun Fact
Boaz was Naomi's family member.

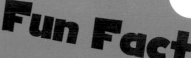

Fun Fact
Ruth traveled with Naomi to Bethlehem. Hundreds of years later, Jesus was born in Bethlehem.

Fun Fact
Ruth had a baby boy named Obed.

Read the Whole Story: Ruth 1–4

Hannah

Hannah believed in the power of prayer. Hannah prayed whenever she was sad or worried.

Hannah wanted to be a mom. She prayed
with all her heart for a baby boy. Hannah
prayed until tears fell from her eyes.

Hannah prayed until a priest named
Eli noticed her.
Hannah told Eli, "I'm sad. I was
telling God about my troubles." Eli
told Hannah to go in peace.

God heard Hannah's prayers and gave
her a baby boy. Hannah named him
Samuel.

Takeaway:
God answers prayers. Talk to God
about things that matter to you.

*I prayed for this child. The L*ORD
has given me what I asked him for.
—1 Samuel 1:27

Prayer:
Dear God, thank you for answering
my prayers. Amen.

Fun Fact
God blessed Hannah with five more children.

Fun Fact
Hannah wrote a beautiful song to thank God for her son. Read her song in 1 Samuel 2.

Fun Fact
Hannah's husband was named Elkanah. He loved Hannah very much.

Read the Whole Story: 1 Samuel 1–2

David

David was the greatest king of Israel.
David knew everything he had was a
gift from God. David told everyone
that God was his strength.

When David was young, he defeated a giant named Goliath. David gave God all the credit for his victory.

God saved David from King Saul.
God kept David safe again and again.
David thanked God for protecting him.

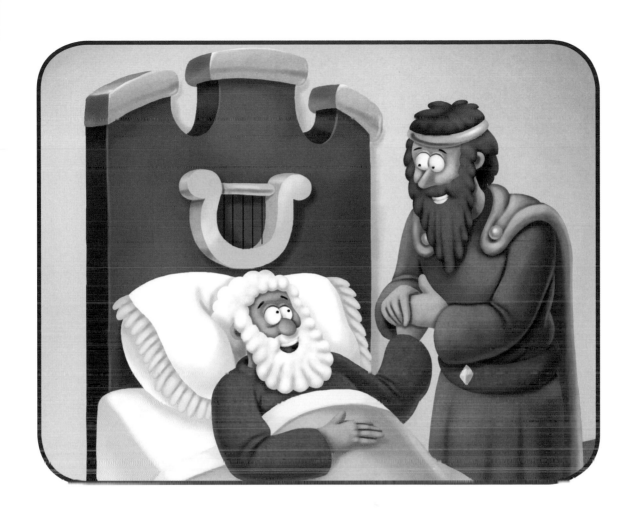

David ruled Israel for 40 years. Even
when David was old and dying, he talked
about all the ways God had blessed him.

Takeaway:
Thank God for all the ways he
helps you.

*"You are coming to fight against
me with a sword, a spear and a
javelin. But I'm coming against
you in the name of the LORD who
rules over all."*—1 Samuel 17:45

Prayer:
Dear God, I can't do anything
without you. Thank you for all the
ways you help me. Amen.

Fun Fact
David wrote more than 70 songs about God. They are called psalms.

Fun Fact
David's best friend was King Saul's son, Jonathan.

Fun Fact
David played the harp.

Read the Whole Story: 1 Samuel 17–1 Kings 2

Solomon

When King David died, David's son
Solomon became king. Solomon was
the wisest man there ever was.

God came to Solomon in a dream. God told him, "You can ask for whatever you want."

Solomon didn't ask for power, riches, or fame. Instead, Solomon asked for wisdom. He wanted to be a good king. He wanted to take care of God's people. God was happy with Solomon's choice.

God gave Solomon great wisdom.
Solomon knew about animals, math,
plants, business, laws, love, and all
kinds of things.

Visitors came from everywhere to ask
Solomon for wise advice.

Takeaway:
God will give you wisdom if you
ask for it. He will help you make
the best decisions.

*"So give me a heart that
understands. Then I can rule
over your people. I can tell the
difference between what is right
and what is wrong." —1 Kings 3:9*

Prayer:
Dear God, please give me wisdom
to know right from wrong. I want
to live for you. Amen.

Fun Fact

Solomon built a beautiful temple for God. He made it out of cedar wood and gold.

Fun Fact

Solomon wrote 3,000 proverbs, or wise sayings. He also wrote over 1,000 songs!

Fun Fact

Solomon ruled Israel for 40 years.

Read the Whole Story: 1 Kings 3–11

Elijah

Elijah loved God. But most people were worshiping a fake god named Baal.

Elijah was the only prophet of the one
true God. Elijah felt alone, but he stayed
faithful to God.

Elijah wanted to show everyone who
the real God was. Elijah told the
people to build an altar to Baal. Elijah
built an altar to God. Elijah said,
"You pray to Baal. I'll pray to God.
Whoever answers with fire is real."

Nothing happened to Baal's altar. But
God's altar burst into flames.
The people fell to their knees. They said,
"The LORD is God."

Takeaway:
Even when others don't follow God, you can stay close to God.

*"Answer me. L*ORD*, answer me. Then these people will know that you are the one and only God. They'll know that you are turning their hearts back to you again."* —1 Kings 18:37

Prayer:
Dear God, please help me stay close to you, no matter what anyone else says or does. Amen.

Fun Fact

When Elijah hid from a mean king, God gave Elijah water from a stream to drink. God even sent birds to bring him food.

Fun Fact

Another time, God gave Elijah fresh-baked bread and a jar of water.

Fun Fact

Read another story about Elijah in Matthew 17.

Read the Whole Story: 1 Kings 17–19

The Widow Helps Elijah

A widow and her son were very poor.
But the widow was still willing to
share with others.

Elijah asked the widow for some water.
The widow shared her water with Elijah.

Then Elijah asked the widow for some bread. The widow told Elijah, "I only have a little flour in my bowl and a little oil in my jar." She only had enough to make one last meal for herself and her son.

But the widow shared with Elijah anyway.

God blessed the widow for helping others. God made sure the widow and her son never went hungry.

Takeaway:
You can always share with others, because God will give you exactly what you need.

The jar of flour wasn't used up. The jug always had oil in it. —1 Kings 17:16

Prayer:
Dear God, thank you for food, water, life, and all the ways you care for me. Amen.

Fun Fact
The widow and her son lived in a town called Zarephath.

Fun Fact
When the widow's son got sick, Elijah prayed to God, and God healed the boy.

Fun Fact
The kind of oil the woman kept in her jar was olive oil.

Read the Whole Story: 1 Kings 17:8–24

Josiah

Josiah became king when he was only eight years old. Josiah always tried to obey God.

Josiah's workers found a scroll that had
been lost for many years. The scroll was
the Book of the Law. God's people had
lost the laws God gave them.

Josiah was sad the people had
forgotten God's laws. So Josiah read
the scroll to all of his people.

Then, Josiah promised to always obey
God. He had his people promise to obey
God too. God was pleased with Josiah
and took care of him.

*There was no king like Josiah
either before him or after him.
None of them turned to the LORD
as he did. He obeyed the LORD with
all his heart and all his soul. He
obeyed him with all his strength.*
—2 Kings 23:25

Prayer:
Dear God, please help me do
my best to please you every day.
Amen.

Fun Fact

Josiah restored the temple Solomon built.

Fun Fact

The people had many temples and statues. They used them to worship fake gods. Josiah got rid of them all!

Fun Fact

Josiah reminded the people to start celebrating the Passover holiday again.

Read the Whole Story: 2 Kings 22–23

Esther

God took Esther to a new place where
she could make a huge difference.

King Xerxes was looking for a new queen.
He picked Esther. Esther didn't know how
to live in a palace or be a queen.

When God's people were in danger,
Esther wanted to help them. She was
nervous. But God made Esther the
queen so she could save God's people.

Esther was afraid, but she begged King
Xerxes to save her people. King Xerxes
agreed. God's people were saved because
Esther was brave.

Takeaway:
God put you where you are so you
can do great things.

*"Who knows? It's possible that
you became queen for a time just
like this." —Esther 4:14*

Prayer:
Dear God, please help me serve
you right where I am. Amen.

Fun Fact

Esther got beauty treatments for twelve months before she met the king.

Fun Fact

Esther's cousin, Mordecai, became one of the king's most important helpers.

Fun Fact

Esther was an orphan.

Read the Whole Story: Esther 1–10

Daniel

Daniel was chosen to work for the
king. Daniel wasn't afraid of anything.
He knew God was on his side.

Daniel wasn't afraid to speak up about
the food in the palace. He knew God
didn't want him to eat that food. He
asked for other food instead.

A new law said no one could pray to
God. But Daniel prayed anyway. He
wasn't afraid. He knew talking to God
was a great thing.

Even when he was thrown into the lions'
den, Daniel trusted God. And God kept
Daniel safe.

"Daniel is one of the prisoners from Judah ... He doesn't obey the order you put in writing. He still prays to his God three times a day." —Daniel 6:13

Fun Fact
God sent an angel to protect Daniel from the lions.

Fun Fact
God gave Daniel dreams with messages for the people.

Fun Fact
Daniel prayed to God three times a day.

Read the Whole Story: Daniel 1–6

Jonah

Jonah was a messenger for God. When Jonah didn't trust God's plan, God gave Jonah a second chance.

God told Jonah to go to Nineveh and tell the people to obey God. But he did not want to go to Nineveh.

Instead, Jonah ran away. He got on a boat going in the other direction.

God sent a storm to stop the boat. The sailors were afraid. They threw Jonah overboard.

A giant fish swallowed Jonah. It spit him out on the beach after three days.

God gave Jonah another chance to listen to him. This time, Jonah obeyed.

Takeaway:
God gave Jonah a second chance.
When you make a mistake, God will
always help get you back on track.

*A message from the LORD came to
Jonah a second time. The LORD said,
"Go to the great city of Nineveh.
Announce to its people the message I
give you." —Jonah 3:1–2*

Prayer:
Dear God, thank you for forgiving
me when I mess up. Thank you for
giving me a second chance. Amen.

Fun Fact

Jonah stayed alive in the belly of a huge fish for three days!

Fun Fact

When Jonah was sitting in the hot sun, God grew a leafy plant to give Jonah shade.

Fun Fact

More than 120,000 people lived in Nineveh.

Read the Whole Story: Jonah 1–4

Mary

Mary was Jesus' mom. She was an ordinary young woman, but Mary's life was amazing because Jesus was her son.

An angel told Mary she would have a
baby. Mary's son would save the world.
Mary asked, "How can that be?" But
Mary trusted God.

Shepherds bowed to Mary's baby.
Wise men from far away brought gifts
for him. This did not happen to other
moms and their babies. Mary knew
Jesus was God's son.

Mary took Jesus to the temple to worship
God and pray. Mary watched Jesus grow
up and teach people about God. Mary was
there when Jesus died on the cross. She
cried, but Mary knew Jesus had saved the
world.

Takeaway:
You can be a normal kid, but Jesus can make your life amazing.

"I serve the Lord," Mary answered. "May it happen to me just as you said it would."
—Luke 1:38

Prayer:
Dear God, I am just a normal kid, but you make my life amazing.
Thank you! Amen.

Fun Fact

Mary had other sons and daughters.

Fun Fact

Mary encouraged Jesus to do his first miracle. Jesus turned water into wine at a wedding.

Fun Fact

Mary was a teenager when she married Joseph and gave birth to Jesus.

Read the Whole Story: Matthew 1–2, Luke 1–2, John 2

Jesus

Jesus is God's son. He is the most
powerful King of Kings. Jesus is
also the most loving. He loves every
person on earth.

Jesus came to the world to show
everyone how much God loves them.
Jesus taught people how to love God and
other people.

Jesus calmed storms and healed the sick.

Jesus' friend Lazarus died, but Jesus
brought Lazarus back to life!

Jesus showed people how much he
loved them by eating, praying, and
talking with them.

Jesus died on the cross to clean up our
lives and hearts. He forgives us. Jesus
fixes our broken parts so we can live
with God in heaven forever.

Takeaway:
Jesus loves you so much. He would do anything for you. He even died so you can spend forever with him.

God so loved the world that he gave his one and only Son. Anyone who believes in him will not die but will have eternal life.
—John 3:16

Prayer:
Dear Jesus, thank you for loving me so much. Thank you for coming into the world and dying for me. Amen.

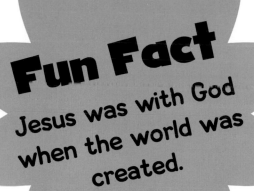

Fun Fact
Jesus was with God when the world was created.

Fun Fact
Before Jesus began preaching he was a carpenter. That's someone who builds things out of wood.

Fun Fact
Jesus visited his disciples many times after he rose from the dead. He ate with them and talked to them.

Read the Whole Story: Matthew, Mark, Luke, John

Anna

Anna was a prophet. She delivered
God's messages to his people. Anna
talked to God all the time.

Anna lived in the temple. She prayed all
day and night.

Mary and Joseph brought baby Jesus to
the temple. Anna knew that Jesus was
God's son right away! Anna recognized
Jesus because she talked to God so often.

Anna was so excited that Jesus had come!
Anna thanked God. She told everyone that
Jesus would save the world.

Takeaway:
When you spend time with God,
you get to know him better.

*She never left the temple. She worshiped
night and day, praying and going
without food. —Luke 2:37*

Prayer:
Dear God, I want to know you
more. Please help me spend more
time with you. Amen.

Fun Fact
Anna lived to be 84 years old.

Fun Fact
Anna's dad was named Phanuel.

Fun Fact
Anna saw Jesus when he was eight days old.

Read the Whole Story: Luke 2:36–38

John the Baptist

John knew Jesus was coming. John taught people about God's love. He wanted them to be ready for Jesus.

John loved God. He wanted people to stop doing bad things. He told them to follow God instead. John lived in the desert and ate bugs and honey. But mostly, John told people about God.

John baptized people from all over.
They got baptized to show others they
wanted to live God's way. John told
people someone special was coming—
Jesus!

Jesus asked John to baptize him in the river.

Takeaway:
You can help others choose good over bad, so they can be ready for Jesus too.

He will teach people who don't obey to be wise and do what is right. In this way, he will prepare a people who are ready for the Lord.
—Luke 1:17

Prayer:
Dear God, please help me help others do the right thing, so they can be ready for you. Amen.

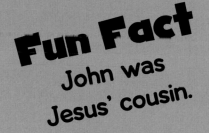

Fun Fact

John was Jesus' cousin.

Fun Fact

700 years before John was born Isaiah said someone would come to get everyone ready for Jesus.

Fun Fact

John wore clothes made of camel hair.

Read the Whole Story: Matthew 3, Mark 1, Luke 1 and 3, John 1

The Disciples

The disciples were Jesus' helpers.
They left everything they had to
follow Jesus.

One day Peter and Andrew were fishing.
Jesus said, "Follow me." So they dropped
their nets and followed him. James and
John were in their boat too. Jesus told
them, "Follow me." So they left their
boat and followed Jesus.

The disciples went everywhere with
Jesus. They listened to Jesus teach and
learned about God's love.

After Jesus went up to heaven, the
disciples traveled around the world. They
taught others about Jesus and his love.

Takeaway:
You can follow Jesus and tell
others about him.

"Come and follow me," Jesus said.
*"I will send you out to fish for
people."* At once they left their nets
and followed him. —Mark 1:17–18

Prayer:
Dear Jesus, I will follow you in all
that I do. Amen.

Fun Fact
Hundreds of people followed Jesus, but Jesus picked twelve to be his closest helpers.

Fun Fact
The 12 disciples were just regular men but Jesus knew they could all do special things.

Fun Fact
Jesus told the disciples to tell everybody about Jesus and his great love after he went to heaven.

Read the Whole Story: Matthew 4, Mark 1, Luke 5–6

The Boy with Fish and Bread

A huge crowd came to listen to Jesus.
They got very hungry. There was a
boy in the crowd. The boy only had
a little bit of food, but he wanted to
share it.

170

The boy had five pieces of bread and two
fish. The boy took the food and gave it
to Jesus.

The boy didn't worry about his own
dinner. He didn't worry if there would
be enough for everyone. The boy gave
what he could, and he trusted Jesus
with the rest.

Jesus used the boy's small meal to feed
thousands of people.

Takeaway:
It doesn't matter how much you have—
Jesus can use it to do great things!

"Here is a boy with five small loaves of barley bread. He also has two small fish. But how far will that go in such a large crowd?"
—John 6:9

Prayer:
Dear Jesus, please help me share what I have. I trust you to do great things. Amen.

Fun Fact

There were twelve baskets of leftovers after everyone ate!

Fun Fact

Five thousand men were in the crowd, plus women and kids. They all ate until they were full!

Fun Fact

The crowd sat down on a grassy hill to eat.

Read the Whole Story: John 6:5–15

The Good Samaritan

The Good Samaritan helped others.

The Samaritan man was traveling from one town to another. He saw a Jewish man who was hurt and lying at the side of the road. Other people had seen the hurt man too, but they did not stop.

The Good Samaritan wanted to help!
So, he cleaned up the man's wounds
and put bandages on them.

The Good Samaritan put the man on
his own donkey and took him to an inn.
Then he took care of the man and paid
for his food. He was so kind and giving!

Takeaway:
Jesus wants us to help others.

Love your neighbor as you love yourself. —Luke 10:27

Prayer:
Dear Jesus, please help me treat others kindly. Amen.

Fun Fact

A priest and a temple helper passed the hurt man, but they didn't help.

Fun Fact

Samaritans and Jewish people did not like each other. But the Good Samaritan helped the hurt man anyway!

Fun Fact

Jesus told this story to show us how to love others.

Read the Whole Story: Luke 10:25–37

Mary and Martha

Mary and Martha were sisters who loved Jesus. Mary and Martha did different things to show their love for Jesus.

One day, Jesus came to visit Mary and Martha. Martha made sure the house was clean, the table was set, and dinner was cooked for Jesus. She was very busy!

Mary sat by Jesus and listened to everything he said.

Martha got angry at Mary. Martha wanted Mary to help with the chores. But Jesus reminded Martha that spending time with him is the most important thing to do.

Takeaway:
Spending time with Jesus is the
most important thing.

*"Martha, Martha," the Lord
answered. "You are worried and
upset about many things ...
Really, only one thing is needed.
Mary has chosen what is better."*
—Luke 10:41-42

Prayer:
Dear Jesus, I love to spend time
with you. You are the most
important thing. Amen.

Fun Fact

Mary and Martha lived in a town called Bethany.

Fun Fact

Mary and Martha's brother, Lazarus, is the man Jesus raised from the dead.

Fun Fact

Martha was older than her sister, Mary.

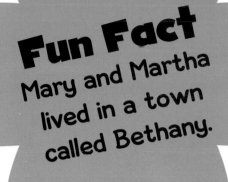

Read the Whole Story: Luke 10:38–42, John 11:17–44

The Prodigal Son

The prodigal son was selfish. He wanted to have fun no matter what the cost.

The son didn't care about anyone else's
feelings. He took the money his dad
saved for him and left home. He spent all
the money on things he wanted to buy.
All he cared about was himself.

Then the prodigal son ran out of money. He was hungry, cold, and lonely. He realized what a mess he'd made. He wanted to make things better. So he went home to tell his dad how sorry he was.

The son could not believe it when his
father ran out and hugged him! His father
loved him no matter what.

Takeaway:
Jesus told this story to show us how much God loves us. God loves us even when we make mistakes.

"He was filled with tender love for his son. He ran to him. He threw his arms around him and kissed him." —Luke 15:20

Prayer:
Dear God, thank you for loving me. Please forgive me when I mess up. Amen.

Fun Fact

When the prodigal son came home, his father gave him a fancy robe and expensive ring.

Fun Fact

The father gave the prodigal son 1/3 of his money. The older son got the other 2/3.

Fun Fact

When the prodigal son ran out of money, he lived with pigs and ate pig food. Ick!

Read the Whole Story: Luke 15:11–31

The Ten Lepers

Ten men had a terrible skin sickness.
It was called leprosy.

The ten lepers had to stay away from
healthy people. They felt lonely.

The ten lepers believed Jesus could heal them. When they saw Jesus the men called out, "Jesus, save us!"

Jesus came to talk to the lepers. The
lepers felt loved and important.
Then Jesus healed them. He changed
their lives forever.

Takeaway:
Jesus loves you. He can change
your life!

*Then Jesus said to him, "Get up
and go. Your faith has healed
you." —Luke 17:19*

Prayer:
Dear Jesus, thank you for always
loving me. You make me feel
special. Amen.

Fun Fact
Only one of the men Jesus healed came back to thank him.

Fun Fact
Lots of people were mean to lepers. People called them names and threw things at them.

Fun Fact
The leper who thanked Jesus was a Samaritan.

Read the Whole Story: Luke 17:11–17

Children

Jesus loved spending time with children.

Children loved to spend time with Jesus too. They crowded around him.

The disciples tried to shoo the children away. They thought Jesus was too busy.

Jesus told the disciples, "Let the children come to me." Jesus wanted to be with the children. The children felt happy, special, and loved.

Takeaway:
Jesus loves children—including you!
Jesus always has time for you.

Jesus said, "Let the little children come to me. Don't keep them away. The kingdom of heaven belongs to people like them."
—Matthew 19:14

Prayer:
Dear Jesus, thank you for spending time with me. Thank you for reminding me how special I am. Amen.

Fun Fact

Parents brought their children to Jesus. Jesus would bless the children.

Fun Fact

The disciples asked Jesus who the most important person in heaven was. Jesus showed them a child.

Fun Fact

Jesus warned grownups not to bring danger to children.

Read the Whole Story: Matthew 18:2–5, 19:13–15, Mark 10:13–16, Luke 18:15–17

Zacchaeus

Before he met Jesus, Zacchaeus
was a greedy man. Jesus changed
Zacchaeus's heart.

Zacchaeus wanted to see Jesus, but he
was too short to see over the crowd. So
Zacchaeus climbed a tree to see Jesus
better.

Jesus saw Zacchaeus in the tree.
Jesus called up to Zacchaeus and
said he would come over for dinner.
Zacchaeus could not believe Jesus
wanted to spend time with him!

Zacchaeus felt loved. He wanted to
change his ways. Zacchaeus stopped
being greedy.

Takeaway:
Jesus always sees you. He loves you, no matter what you have done.

"The Son of Man came to look for the lost and save them."
—Luke 19:10

Prayer:
Dear Jesus, thank you for seeing me no matter where I am. Thank you for loving me always. Amen.

Fun Fact

The tree Zacchaeus climbed was a sycamore-fig tree.

Fun Fact

Zacchaeus gave the people back four times as much money as he took.

Fun Fact

Zacchaeus's job was to collect taxes. He cheated people by taking extra money.

Read the Whole Story: Luke 19:1–10

Poor Widow

At the temple, Jesus saw a widow. Her husband had died, and she was very poor.

The widow wondered how she could give anything to God's temple. She only had a couple of coins.

The poor widow believed God would take care of her needs. She decided to give two coins. That was everything she had.

Jesus noticed the generous widow. He told his disciples about her faith and trust in God.

Takeaway:
Jesus notices when you share what you have.

"They all gave a lot because they are rich. But she gave even though she is poor. She put in everything she had. That was all she had to live on." —Mark 12:44

Prayer:
Dear Jesus, everything I have comes from you. Please help me share freely. Amen.

Fun Fact
Jesus and the widow were in a part of the temple called the Court of Women.

Fun Fact
The widow gave two copper coins. These were worth a couple of pennies.

Fun Fact
There were seven offering boxes in this area of the temple.

Read the Whole Story: Mark 12:41–44, Luke 21:1–4

Paul

Saul didn't know much about Jesus. When Saul met Jesus, his entire life changed.

Jesus chose Saul to tell others how much
Jesus loves them.

Saul was so excited to share Jesus'
love. Jesus changed Saul's name to
Paul. Paul spent the rest of his life
traveling all over the world. He told
everyone about Jesus.

Paul listened to people's stories. Then
he told them how Jesus could make their
lives better.

Takeaway:
Jesus has chosen you to show others how much he loves them.

"Go! I have chosen this man to work for me. He will announce my name to the Gentiles and to their kings." —Acts 9:15

Prayer:
Dear Jesus, thank you for choosing me. Please help me share your great love with others. Amen.

Fun Fact

Paul was blind for three days after he met Jesus.

Fun Fact

Paul wrote letters to many churches and Christians. Thirteen of these letters are now books of the Bible!

Fun Fact

Paul was a tentmaker.

Read the Whole Story: Acts 9, 13–28, Romans, 1 and 2 Corinthians, Galatians, Ephesians, Colossians, Philippians, Philemon, 1 and 2 Thessalonians, 1 and 2 Timothy, Titus

The Beginner's Bible®

The bestselling Bible storybook of our time—over 25 million sold!

978-0-310-75013-0
$16.99 / Hardcover

The Beginner's Bible® has been a favorite with young children and their parents since its release in 1989 with over 25 million products sold. Now it's redesigned with fresh new art that will excite children for many more years to come.

Full of faith and fun, *The Beginner's Bible®* is a wonderful gift for any child. The easy-to-read text and bright, full-color illustrations on every page make it a perfect way to introduce young children to the stories and characters of the Bible. With new vibrant three-dimensional art and compelling text, more than 90 Bible stories come to life. Kids ages 6 and under will enjoy the fun illustrations of Noah helping the elephant onto the ark, Jonah praying inside the fish, and more, as they discover *The Beginner's Bible®* just like millions of children before. *The Beginner's Bible®* was named the 2006 Retailers Choice Award winner in Children's Nonfiction.

Check out these other products featuring The Beginner's Bible.®

978-0-310-75957-7

978-0-310-76030-6

978-0-310-76111-2

978-0-310-75979-9

978-0-310-75955-3

978-0-310-75704-7

978-0-310-75701-6

978-0-310-75536-4

978-0-310-75610-1